Josef Herman in his studio

Josef Herman in Wales

Carolyn Davies

pont
library

First Impression—2001
Second Impression—2004

ISBN 1 85902 999 X

© Paintings: Josef Herman estate and owners
   as noted.

Carolyn Davies has asserted her right under the
Copyright, Designs and Patents Act, 1988, to be
identified as Author of the text.

All rights reserved. No part of this book may be
reproduced, stored in a retrieval system, or
transmitted in any form or by any means,
electronic, electrostatic, magnetic tape,
mechanical, photocopying, recording or
otherwise without permission in writing from
the publishers, Pont Books, Gomer Press,
Llandysul, Ceredigion.

Printed in Wales at
Gomer Press, Llandysul, Ceredigion

Acknowledgement

The author and publishers gratefully acknowledge the
support and help received in preparing this publication.
Special thanks are due to Nini Herman for her
generosity and enthusiasm; and to the galleries and
other owners of the works.

The photograph on page 2 is by permission of David
Herman.
The photographs on pages 28 and 31 are by
Llew E. Morgan.
The artist's own words are taken from *Notes from a
Welsh Diary* by Josef Herman, published in 1988 by
Free Association Books, and reproduced here by kind
permission of Nini Herman.

Untitled (Landscape with Road)

Josef Herman, the artist, took his inspiration from nature and the world around him. He would note the smallest movement, the slightest change or shift in the light. He loved colour, observing every different shade of the passing seasons.

Untitled (Tree in Landscape)

Josef had a special way of painting. He took notes from nature and drew and painted from memory. With closed eyes, he simplified what he saw. He would leave out the details that were not essential, and concentrate instead on shape and form. His images are bold and sculptural.

Untitled (Blue Bird)

His memory fed his imagination.

The bird, the coal miner, the tree; these are among his favourite subjects. He painted and drew them again and again but each time with a different line, different tone or different shape.

Untitled (Road and Mountain with figures)

Josef Herman was born in Poland. When he was a young man he moved to Belgium and France and, then with the threat of war, he moved again. This time his travels took him to Scotland and eventually to Wales.

Autumn 1946

He came to the Swansea Valley and settled in the village of Ystradgynlais.

He lived there for eleven years and he was happy. 'I stayed because here I found ALL I required. I arrived a stranger for a fortnight. The fortnight became eleven years,' he said.

Evening, Ystradgynlais

Untitled (Ystradgynlais)

10

He loved the valley, the river and the hills. 'I walked the small streets and the open hills where you can touch the sky,' said Josef.

He spent days just looking. He loved the colours he saw. In his diary he wrote about, 'the red landscape, the bright green horizon'.

Untitled (Village Rooftops)

The night was illuminated with 'green stars in black deeps and a full yellow moon'.

In the village he saw 'grey light and gold over the rooftops'.

Three Miners

The thick rain was like 'yellow syrup', and often the valley could only be seen through 'the white fog and the pale green mist'.

The Tip 1973

For Josef, the village was full of fascinating shapes: 'the road shining like a window, the coal tip a black pyramid in the sky.'

The river running through the valley was silent and green, as smooth as grass.

Untitled (Yellow and Black Trees in Landscape)

'The River Tawe', said Josef, 'has always two colours more than the sky – blackness of coal and yellow of clay.'

The trees were glazed with light.

Untitled (Goat)

He watched life all around him, the ducks on the road, goats along the canal, swallows in the sky.

Untitled (Two Ponies)

In the severe winter he saw the hungry ponies who came down from the distant hills, standing still in twos or threes, mostly at garden gates, their breath white.

Untitled (Landscape with Two Ponies and Woman)

In his diary, Josef often described the people who looked after the animals.

'The women, old and young, with baskets filled with leftovers, boiled potatoes, bread, carrots. The children laughing and singing Welsh songs, following the ponies everywhere…'

Two Miners II

Josef enjoyed a cup of tea with his neighbour, Dai Dan, and went walking with his friend, Llew.

Many of Josef's friends were miners who lived in the village. He would hear their hobnailed boots on the road as they passed his window in the dark on their way to work.

He was pleased when they would look up to his light and lift an arm in greeting.

Miners Singing

The people of the village called him Joe Bach. In his paintings, he portrayed them with affection:

'... Mrs Hodge with a sieve, Willie with a spade, a pile of coal for winter in front of the cottage ...

'. . . the miners arriving on the brown bus . . . the long queue at the fish and chip shop . . . the young men and women singing into space . . .'

Mother and Child

'the mother with child in her patterned Welsh shawl . . . the young man with a cage of restless pigeons. Women washing the pavements near their homes.'

Josef painted them all.

Untitled (Miner Bathing)

    Wherever he went, his interest in people was always there. 'Being interested in people, I draw people,' said Josef.

Miners (Mural)

But it was the workers that inspired him most. The sight of the miners returning home, silhouetted against the full body of the sun affected Josef greatly. The miners came unexpectedly, as though from nowhere, stepping on to the bridge.

For a split second, with the light around them and the yellow disc of the sun behind their heads, Josef thought that they looked like saints, with their haloes glowing.

Miner on Bridge

The magnificence of the miners on the bridge he found overwhelming. The scene stayed with him forever.

It was an image that kept Wales alive for him and it remained significant throughout his working life.

Untitled (Yellow Tree and Two Figures)

Josef Herman never stopped painting. Every day, he drew, right to the end of his life.

'Work goes on', he said. 'I will go on working, of course; with me working is living.'

About the Artist's Life

1911	Born in Warsaw, Poland on 3 January
1930	Enrols at Warsaw School of Art and Decoration. Leaves after 18 months to work as a graphic artist.
1931	First exhibition in Warsaw.
1938	Leaves Poland for Belgium and then France.
1940	Arrives in Britain and settles in Glasgow.
1941	Exhibits in Glasgow and Edinburgh.
1944	Visits Ystradgynlais and stays.
1946	Holds first one man show of Welsh pastels and drawings in London.
1949	Exhibits in London.
1950	Commissioned to paint a mural for the Festival of Britain (now in the Glynn Vivian Art Gallery, Swansea)
1955	Moves to London.
1955 onwards	Regular exhibitions in Britain and abroad.

Josef Herman sketching miners at the coalface

1961	Moved to Suffolk where he and his wife bring up their young family.
1962	Awarded Gold Medal by the National Eisteddfod, for his services to Welsh Art.
1972	Moves from Suffolk to West London where he lived for the rest of his life.
1975	Publishes his autobiography *Related Twilights*.
1981	Awarded OBE for his services to British Art.
1990	Becomes a Royal Academician.
1991	Retrospective Exhibition, National Museum of Wales, Cardiff. Awarded the International Medallion for services to art by the Contemporary Art Society for Wales.
1999	Launches book *Song of the Migrant Bird* and exhibits lithographs from the book at the Royal Academy, London.
2000	Dies in London aged 89

Untitled

Where to see Josef Herman's work

Arts Council of Britain, England, Wales
Contemporary Arts Society, London and Wales
Glynn Vivian Art Gallery, Swansea
National Museum of Wales, Cardiff
The British Council
Tate Gallery, London
Victoria and Albert Museum, London
Galleries in the major cities in Wales, England, Scotland and Northern Ireland
Galleries in: New Zealand, South Africa, Canada, Australia, Germany, Israel

Details of the paintings

Front Cover: Untitled
Pastel on Paper
25 x 20 cms

Page 5   Untitled (Landscape with Road)
Watercolour
19.5 x 25 cms

Page 6   Untitled (Tree in Landscape)
Pastel

Page 7   Untitled (Blue Bird)
Watercolour
14 x 14.5 cms

Page 8   Untitled (Road and Mountain with figures)
Watercolour
20 x 20 cms

Page 9   Autumn 1946
Pastel
50 x 63 cms

Page 10   Untitled (Ystradgynlais) 1957
Pencil and Pen and Ink Wash on Paper
20 x 25 cms

Page 11   Evening, Ystradgynlais 1958/59
Oil on Canvas 63.5 x 85 cms
Tate Gallery, London

Page 12   Untitled (Village Rooftops)
Pastel on Paper
25 x 20 cms

Page 13   Three Miners 1956
Oil on Wood
34.5 x 52 cms
Tate Gallery, London

Page 14   The Tip 1973
Oil on Board
43.5 x 61.5 cms
Angela Flowers Gallery, London

Page 15   Untitled (Yellow and Black Trees in Landscape)
Watercolour
25 x 20 cms

Page 16   Untitled (Goat)
         Pen and Ink wash on paper
         12.2 x 14 cms

Page 17   Untitled (Two Ponies)
         Mixed Media on Paper
         19 x 23 cms

Page 18   Untitled
         (Landscape with Two Ponies and Woman)
         Pen and Ink Wash
         20 x 25 cms

Page 19   Two Miners II
         Pen and Ink Wash
         19 x 23 cms
         Collection Carolyn Davies

Page 20   Miners Singing 1950 –51
         Oil
         43.5 x 121.6 cms
         National Museum and Gallery of Wales

Page 22   Mother and Child 1945 – 50
         Oil on Board
         89 x 72.5 cms
         Glynn Vivian Art Gallery

Page 23   Untitled (Miner Bathing)
         Pen and Ink Wash
         24 x 16 cms
         Collection Mike Jones

Page 24   Miners
         Festival of Britain Mural Panels 1951
         Oil on Board
         132.4 x 281.6 cms
         Glynn Vivian Art Gallery

Page 26   Miner on Bridge 1945
         Oil on Canvas
         Angela Flowers Gallery, London

Page 27   Untitled (Yellow Tree and Two Figures) 1985-86
         Oil on Board
         90 x 103 cms
         Angela Flowers Gallery, London

Page 29   Untitled
         Pen and Ink Wash
         20 x 25 cms

Josef Herman sketching

31